POP PEOPLE

PHOTOGRAPHS BY **Harry Hammond**

SIDGWICK & JACKSON

LONDON

**For my dear wife Margaret
and our daughter Carole Linda**

First published in 1984 in Great Britain
by Sidgwick and Jackson Limited

Copyright©1984 by Harry Hammond

Designed by David Fuller

Acknowledgements
I would like to thank the following people
and organizations for their kind co-operation
over the years:
Sue Davies, Director of the Photographers'
Gallery; the British Broadcasting Corporation;
Radio Luxembourg; Maurice Kinn; and Ilford Ltd.

Page 1: Gene Vincent (1960)
Pages 2-3: Count Basie and his Orchestra (1957).
A one-night stand at the Royal Festival Hall in London

ISBN 0-283-99016-3 (softcover)
ISBN 0-283-99015-5 (hardcover)

Phototypeset by Falcon Graphic Art Ltd
Wallington, Surrey
Printed in Italy by
Amilcare Pizzi s.p.a., Milan
for Sidgwick and Jackson Limited
1 Tavistock Chambers, Bloomsbury Way
London WC1A 2SG

Contents

Introduction

This book begins with the old dance bands because they were what led me to the picture features on pop people that I still do today. My work before the war was photographing society celebrities for the smart glossy journals, and so it seemed natural to pursue this outlet when I went freelance in 1948. As I started to get assignments I covered a variety of subjects – fashion shows by the top couturiers of the time like Hardy Amies and Norman Hartnell for women's magazines, a weekly picture – on the wire – for the *Melbourne Argus*, for which I became the London photographer, and illustrations for stories in children's annuals. This time around I didn't work as a society photographer in a studio. Instead, I found the rich and famous at garden parties, private receptions, race meetings and exclusive night-clubs – and at these functions there would be entertainers; jazz musicians and well-known bandleaders. The daytime haunt of such musical luminaries in those years was Denmark Street in London, where they would look for songs for their next engagement or broadcast, and in following them into 'Tin Pan Alley' as it was known, I discovered new people to photograph – 'pop people'.

Although I received an invaluable studio training, I have never used one since starting to freelance. I like to work on location with a person in their associated environment – in hotel rooms, at home, or backstage at theatres. The period dealt with in this book was before the days of telephoto lenses, automatic cameras and fast film speeds, and prevailing conditions were sometimes more than adverse. It was not unusual to cover a two-hour concert with a half-dozen dark-slide glass plates in one pocket and a few flash bulbs in the other, and if the performer was too far away on stage you just had to get closer. Colour was also experimental then, but even now I prefer to work in black and white as I think this medium has more value for future generations; most colour prints will not last well into the next century. And I enjoy the extra challenge of working in monochrome. The pictures that follow show a style of photography and lighting which is vastly different from modern practice. But although I must keep pace with present-day demands, I still sometimes like to work in the old-fashioned way.

The current demand for new sounds in popular music and the hunger for new images is a situation that has always been with us, and it is interesting to note that as far back as the twenties the public were buying recordings of rhythm and blues, which is basically rock 'n' roll music. So the pendulum has swung and returned and people are now buying the same rhythmic pattern of music that their grandparents did all those years ago, except that it is now on cassette and in microgroove and is louder and is called rock music.

I would like this book to illustrate a little of the activity that I witnessed in the world of Pop People between 1948 and 1963. The successes and failures, the fortunes won or lost on the turn of a sheet of music or a demo disc, the struggles for survival and the easy slides to stardom. The attempts to introduce new styles for commercial gain or for egoism, the fluctuating tastes and fickle demands of the younger generation and the endless searching for something new. For many years I was the only photographer to produce this type of work, and most of the artistes are shown here at the peak of their professional careers — I hope that this is how they would like to be remembered. This book is a pictorial reminiscence rather than a chronological history, but I have written an introductory page to each of the sections in order to show the different stages in the great changes that took place. It deals with a period which has influenced the present-day world of popular music more than any other — a lens-eye chronicle of the first Pop People.

Prelude to Pop

In the first half of this century there were many different kinds of bands – big, small, brass, jazz, ragtime – but the bands of renown are those of the thirties and forties: the bands of the dance halls and plush hotels; the bands of bebop, ballads and swing, and that 'other new-fangled thing' – radio. As vaudeville and the variety stage declined in popularity during this period, bands became the only means by which an aspiring songwriter could try out his work on the general public. For the public, drooping from the depression years and then the Second World War, a personal appearance (known as a 'gig' or 'one night stand') of a famous bandleader with his musicians at the local ballroom would mean not only escapism but a chance for the devotees to demonstrate their veneration of the bandleader.

The band's main function was to play for dancing, but usually, as the evening progressed, the dancers would start to assemble in front of the stage until several thousand stood before the band and the occasion developed into a kind of swinging promenade concert. The big attraction was always the leader or maestro: impeccably dressed, he wielded his baton with military authority, bouncing up and down in front of his musicians and enjoying the adulation of those unknown but very necessary people who later, in another age, would be called 'fans'.

Seated to one side of the musicians at a dutiful distance, unnoticed until they were commanded to stand up and present, mechanically, the current popular tune, were the real ambassadors of song – the band singers.

Such bands and orchestras as these can be seen on the next few pages. Some immortalized their musical sounds on wax, others never recorded a single note in the whole of their existence. But this is how it was, in the beginning.

Eric Delaney (1954). A show drummer, photographed literally
'on tymps' at the Royal Albert Hall in London.
Delaney and his band toured extensively and were an enormous draw

Ivy Benson and her All Girls Band (1951). They played a different city every
night of the week in an endless display of fashion and brilliant
musicianship, and were the greatest show on the road at the time

Dorothy Squires (1959). A volatile but greatly
talented band singer who has had a continuing
modest success on record. In the seventies she hired
the London Palladium for one night to give her own
concert; there was standing room only.
She repeated the success with Carnegie Hall in New York

Mantovani and his Orchestra (1949). The only known photograph in existence
of the original 'tumbling strings' whose recording of 'Charmaine'
in 1951 sold two million copies, and is still selling today

Above: Ambrose and his Orchestra (1951). Bert Ambrose, an idol of the big band days, launched many of his band singers into successful careers of their own. Here he is fronting the reed section at London's Mayfair Hotel, where he played for many years. Tubby Hayes is on the right

Right: Harry Gold and his Pieces of Eight (1952). Harry and his brother Laurie, pictured here centre and bottom right, ran one of the most successful and entertaining small bands of the dance hall days. The likeable brothers totted up some thirty years on the road and on the air, to the delight of audiences and fellow musicians equally

Edmundo Ros and his Orchestra (1950). Payola was coming
to an end and the music business was entering a new era,
with gramophone records starting to replace sheet music.
Ros had already chalked up big sales with 78s like 'Wedding
Samba' and was putting Latin-American music on the map. Here he
is playing at the fashionable Bagatelle club in Mayfair

Basil Kirchin (1953). An explosive
drummer who, with his father, ran
a very popular small band called,
not very inventively, The Kirchins

Overleaf: BBC Show Band (1954)
Formed in 1952 and directed by
Cyril Stapleton, the Show Band
was a platform for a lot of
international artistes early
in their careers. A young Petula
Clark and Pete Murray are seen
here with Charlie Chester
at the old Paris Cinema
in Lower Regent Street, London

16

Jack Parnell (1954). Uncle Val Parnell, who owned the London Palladium, was helpful when Jack started out on his long career. His first band, The Music Makers, featured Ronnie Scott and other such jazz giants, and also a double drumming show with Phil Seaman. A packed Royal Albert Hall was the venue in this photograph taken at a concert featuring many bands of the day

Woody Herman (1953). One of several American bands touring
United States military bases in the UK at this period. For many
years no overseas musicians were allowed to play in British
venues (the US bases did not count as such) and vice versa
because of union disagreement, but this deadlock was eventually
broken in 1956 with the 'exchange of bands' arrangement

Stan Kenton (1956). With his
wife Ann at the Royal Albert Hall
where he and his full orchestra
appeared in concert to much
acclaim. A unique experience

Johnny Dankworth (1953). A quiet, reserved man but a gifted musician, he
is now a revered musical director and concert celebrity. In this photograph
he is seen blowing at Studio 51 in London with Leon Calvert on the right

Ted Heath and his Orchestra (1955). Success came slowly for the former Geraldo trombonist. With his wife Myra he wrote a song called 'That Lovely Weekend' and financed his first band with the royalties he earned from it. In the early fifties he played to capacity crowds every Sunday in concerts at the London Palladium and his records sold in large numbers. In 1963 he won the Carl Alan Award *(left)* for his outstanding contribution to popular music

Right: Lita Roza (1953). She was a featured vocalist with the Ted Heath Orchestra. Dennis Lotis and Dickie Valentine completed a legendary line-up of vocalists whose original recordings are still much sought after

Don Lusher (1957). The man who helps keep the Ted Heath Orchestra story alive today. He was the original lead trombone player, and today directs a 'gathering of the greats' in concert to re-create those unmistakeable sounds

Joe Loss (1963). The incomparable maestro with his Carl
Alan Award. A top band leader for half a century, his
orchestra is constantly in demand today and his
personal appearances are no less amiable and professional than they
were when he first conducted his musicians for 'In The Mood'

The American Invasion

The fifteen years from 1948 to 1963 produced more changes, more longer lasting and varied talent and more sociological reforms than any other time in the history of popular music. In those early years big bands were still popular and a few would remain so, with distinctive sounds like the belting brass of Stan Kenton and Ted Heath, the sloping saxes of Billy May, the strict tempo of Victor Sylvester, or the waterfall violins of Mantovani. But the end was in sight for the majority as this same period introduced the beginning of an unprecedented 'invasion' of Britain by an abundance of American solo vocalists. Their recording success in America led them to view the UK as a likely touring ground for the promotion of further sales of 78s.

As England had no published hit parade then there was no way of being able to ascertain which of all the tender declarations of intent and expressions of love, or frustration, was selling best. But if a chart could be compiled and published it would lead to even more sales of the favoured waxing. This in turn would pinpoint the most 'popular' record, song or singer, and eventually lead to 'pop' music and 'pop' people.

With this significant and promising idea in mind, the *New Musical Express* began publishing in November 1952 a weekly survey of the 'Top 12 Best-selling Records' in Britain. This list of merit was very quickly inundated with contributions from the above-mentioned boys and girls from across the Atlantic. From then on, the United Kingdom was wide open for personal appearances of these newly ascended solo stars. After a week or so at the London Palladium several weeks of touring the theatre circuit was not unusual – topping the bill over dancers, jugglers, ventriloquists and other variety entertainers.

For the recording industry in both America and Britain these early years were a time of fomentation when the giant companies of today were being forged in a crucible of wax and wire recorders. Innumerable record labels were launched and most of them expanded and had their own legendary success stories to tell. It was the advent of mass platter peddling, and the doyens of disc distribution would never look back.

Billy Daniels (1956). Dynamic is far too mild a word
to describe 'That Ole Black Magic' hit maker. A regular visitor
to England, his performances were breathtaking to watch

Dean Martin (1953). Posing by the London Palladium
piano. A helpful and friendly artiste who has
always known the value of a good publicity photograph

Frank Sinatra (1953). A co-operative camera subject if he knew the
photographer and could rely on the shots being taken quickly with
the minimum of apparatus. I caught him on a radio show with ace
BBC producer Johnny Stewart as he was promoting his first British tour

Johnnie Ray (1953). 'The Prince of Wails': for the first time ever, audiences
could be seen tearing themselves apart. He was the first pop singer to
exploit the mobile image on stage and the picture opposite shows him
demonstrating an idea that The Who would use in their act twenty years later.
This photograph, taken in 1955, shows him (centre) watching buskers in London's
Leicester Square, unnoticed by the crowd, during a break in his own rehearsals

Guy Mitchell (1955). His records were always in the Top Twenty during the fifties – his most famous hit was 'She Wears Red Feathers' – and he visited Britain annually for several years. His musical style reflected his easy-going personality

Opposite
Top left: Al Martino (1952). One of the first Americans to appear in London when his 'Here In My Heart' topped the newly invented British charts. His London agent, Ed Jones, gave him a silver platter; this was before record companies thought of doling out records pressed with gold leaf
Top right: Vic Damone (1955). 'On The Street Where You Live' was one of the first hits for MGM's film star, who is still making records today
Bottom left: Tony Martin (1955). A star of films as well as pop, photographed in an age when teenage girls dressed to look like duplicates of their mothers
Bottom right: Joni James (1956). 'Your Cheatin' Heart' was one of many of the delectable Miss James's records that went gold. Chicago-born, her travelling was usually restricted to the United States, but this photograph was taken in a BBC dressing-room. She attributed much of her success to the then unknown Ray Charles and his Singers who backed her

Patti Page (1955). When this photograph was taken in London
Patti Page had already sold more than ten million singles.
She maintained that it was all due to good publicity

Eddie Fisher (1953). This photograph says it all: a
'king' of the hit parade looks at a new Queen of England

Frankie Laine (1954). One young fan got through when Laine appeared at the
Festival Gardens in London and demonstrated his crowd-pulling power.
One of his many hit records, 'I Believe', stayed in the charts
for three months and brought fame to the ex-waiter from Chicago

Nat King Cole (1954). A jazz singer, pianist and dancer before
moving to pop, this highly talented and charming family man was
a pleasure to photograph and to be with. His recordings need
no explanation and they never date. One of the immortals of pop

Tin Pan Alley

'Tin Pan Alley' in London was really Denmark Street, just off Charing Cross Road and a short cut from Soho to Holborn. It used to be the heart of Britain's 'moon and June' business. It was customary for every music publisher to have an address there, and these clamorous residents thronged every available back room, cellar, office and outhouse – their sole mission in life to promote hit songs.

Up to the middle of the fifties a new song would still be actually written in crotchets and quavers, on a manuscript, with a clef and stave, and inevitably many a hit song started life scribbled on a paper bag in the dairy café down the Alley, and sold for thirty shillings. Of course, not everyone could read and write music, but if a tune had potential, someone had to get it down on paper. The piano was the main method of demonstration, and a good plugger would always have to be ready with his opening line – 'I've got a good song in my pocket'.

The origins of Tin Pan Alley in London – or in New York, for that matter – are unknown, but it is thought that Lawrence Wright (who wrote his songs under the name Horatio Nichols) founded the London Alley in 1911 when he hawked song copies from a handcart there. He later rented a room for £1 a week and stayed there for nearly fifty years, producing an endless stream of international hit songs.

Elton Box and Sonny Cox (Box & Cox) started a publishing business there in the forties in an old paint shed and soon notched up a million sales in sheet music with 'Galway Bay'.

Dave Toff, another music publisher extraordinaire who later settled in the Alley, created the first disco in 1930 when he gave free concerts at the Majestic, Tottenham Court Road, of 'Hot Gramophone Records' imported from America. His subsequent achievements included publishing many of Doris Day's hit songs and the theme music for *Coronation Street*.

Bustling with band leaders, music publishers, singers, musicians, pluggers – British and American – this little street witnessed innumerable musical success stories, and an unrepeatable pageant of talent, even genius. It was the foundation stone of popular music as it is today.

Billie Anthony and Petula Clark (1953). Looking for songs in the Alley

'Hutch' (1950). Remembered for his best-selling version
of 'Begin The Beguine', Hutch was a celebrated cabaret
star and early pop singer well known in Tin Pan Alley

Max Bygraves (1952). In Denmark Street
the tills were ringing to the sound of sheet music

Josh White (1952). The great American
jazz and blues guitarist, captured on a
rare visit to a Denmark Street publisher

Lawrence Wright (1954).
The founder of Tin Pan Alley

Dave Toff (1955). One of the most
successful music publishers in the Alley

The Stargazers (1953). They found all their songs down the Alley and
eventually took 'Broken Wings' to Number 1 – the first British
group to achieve this in the newly formed Top Twelve Hit Parade

Some American visitors
to Tin Pan Alley (1954–1962)

Musical director Nelson Riddle

Henry Mancini *(left)* and David Rose

The famous song-writer Hoagy Carmichael

TV personality Ed Sullivan

Danny Purches (1954). In the early fifties demo-discs were
unknown, but this method was just as good in Tin Pan Alley.
Purches went on to sign a contract worth £100,000 and
won a place in the charts with 'Golden Earrings'

Alma Cogan (1957). The sunny-voiced songstress with the magnificent gowns.
A constant bestseller for EMI regardless of the changing and capricious
demands of the pop world. She found most of her songs in Denmark
Street. I was trying to obstruct the glare of the light behind me when
I caught my reflection in this shot taken on the set of a TV show

Dickie Valentine (1955). The first teenage idol to succeed in Britain,
the prodigious Valentine was already a cult figure in the mid-fifties.
Thousands bought his records and flocked to scream at his dynamic concerts

Joe (Mr Piano) Henderson (1958). A musician of
distinction and an affable inhabitant of Denmark Street

Ronnie Carroll (1957). A product of Tin Pan Alley who was nurtured, as was then the custom, by his record company for several years until the right song was found. The big one came in 1962 with 'Roses Are Red', and Carroll is still a top-line cabaret act today

Tommy Bruce (1957). His gravel voice took him into the
Top Twenty via Denmark Street, but surprisingly after one
hit no more was heard of the porter from London's Covent Garden

Kathy Kirby (1958). Bert Ambrose pointed this attractive band
singer in the right direction, but she never seemed able to cope
with all the traumatic ups and downs of life in Tin Pan Alley

Show Biz and Jazz People

Without *it* a singer is not 'with it' (a logical conclusion), the 'it' being the ability to 'bend' a note or to warp a song into a discord of flat, or sharp, sequences and then glide back to the original key of the song. This need to distort the melody was re-introduced by Ray Charles around 1962 and has remained with every recording vocalist ever since. Descended from gospel singing, it is now heard in pop, country, and rock music, together with suitable physical contortions when presented visually by the singer.

The consequence of this is that to most modern music lovers, bludgeoned into a state of euphoria by a decibal onslaught of pseudo-Afro voices who never hit the note, show business and jazz people seem positively cubic because of their unadulterated rendering of a song. Which prompts the query, why are they included in this treatise of popular artistes? The answer is that there was a time when theatre stars, movie stars, jazz singers and musicians, and comedians made and sold millions of records. It was a time when success on stage, screen or radio would come first – indeed, would be required by many of the recording studios before opening their doors; a reversal of today's situation.

So, by committing their audible image to the worshipful disc, these people became woven into the tapestry of popular music and its heritage and have thus earned their place in this documentary.

Billie Holiday (1954). This legendary lady visited England only
once. This picture and the one overleaf are the only
photographs taken of her on that occasion. I shot this one
during her single performance at the Royal Albert Hall

Billie Holiday (1954). I took this portrait
in her room at London's Piccadilly Hotel

Dizzy Gillespie (1954). A distinctive horn
player, shot behind the tabs at a jazz concert

Georgia Gibbs (1954). An American vocalist whose records sold
big for a time. Here she is onstage at a Royal Albert Hall concert

Lena Horne (1954). 'Stormy Weather' and
''Deed I do' are two of the hundreds of
songs recorded or performed by one of the
world's greatest cabaret artistes. This
picture was taken backstage during her UK tour

Duke Ellington (1957). Onstage at the Royal Festival Hall, London

Norman Wisdom (1955). No mean contributor to his
record company's sales. 'Don't Laugh At Me' is one example

Doris Day (1956). A movie star first and then a million-seller among pop people. An informal shot taken at a party at Claridge's Hotel in London

Ella Fitzgerald (1958). One quick shot selected from many that I took of this peerless lady of jazz whose countless records have been selling for so long

Frankie Vaughan (1956). The Al Jolson style and suave image took
Frank into the best-selling list several times. His ageless appearance
today belies the fact that he has been a star for thirty years

Earl Hines (1959). Seen during a performance
at the Royal Festival Hall with bass player
Jack Lesberg and trombonist Jack Teagarden

The Beverley Sisters (1957). With their girlish style and perfect close-harmony technique, they were probably the last of the 'purity' pop people

Joan Regan (1958). A recording artiste who had a lot of
success in the fifties but never changed her showbiz image

Liberace (1960). A portrait taken at
the Finsbury Park Empire Theatre in
London where, as usual, Liberace
displayed his records prominently on
the stage. Although basically a stage
act, this very friendly and
co-operative star has done more in
this way to promote the sale of
his albums than any other artiste

Cleo Laine (1960). A star whose
jazz-based style and sound
was to take her to the top.
A photograph taken at a
concert between calls on stage

Anthony Newley (1960). His flamboyant talent,
prompted originally by London's Italia Conti Stage
School, soon swept him into films and the
charts. This picture was taken on the set of a TV show

The Low-key Image

It is generally assumed today that popular music is the choice of the majority of people, and that classical music has only a minority following. Also that classical music is inspiring and educational, whilst popular music is decadent and dangerous: the refined and clear-cut, as opposed to the shallow and romantic. This theory may or may not be true, but on closer examination of the two cultures, there is a wider gap that becomes apparent – the visual aspect.

When thousands of admirers flock to the big concert halls to listen to, for example, Claudio Arrau, they are content to watch him working onstage in white tie and tails for the whole show. This static display would also apply to any great tenor in 'action', and the same audience will happily buy huge quantities of their idol's LPs that bear just a portrait on the cover.

For fans of popular music – who are not necessarily all under twenty years old – seeing their favourites is very often more important than hearing them. They expect the singer or musician of their choice to present their music with appropriate posturings and gyrations punctuating every note and lyric. A rousing image generates excitement and interest in a live audience, which indicates to the record company executives that sales could be encouraged if the visual aspect is exploited. Examples of this 'look before you buy' technique were the emaciated Sinatra of the forties, the erotic Presley of the fifties, the ill-mannered Stones of the sixties, and the depraved Sex Pistols of the seventies. All artfully contrived images and all used with one intent – to help sell records.

But there was also an era when the image was not so important – when record-buyers purchased millions of pressings without ever having seen the artistes, unless they were movie stars. The whole operation was based on a combination of vocal or instrumental ability and that elusive hit song. Overleaf are some images of pop people who fell into this category in the fifties and early sixties, but who will be remembered for a long time, for all that!

The Hi Los (1956). Their harmony sold
this slick Canadian group to record-buyers

Eddie Calvert (1954). His giant single 'Oh
Mein Papa' sold nearly four million copies

Connie Francis (1958). One of the first
girl singers to develop a rock sound. A
lovely lady who was a delight to photograph

Burl Ives (1953). Well known for 'Little Bitty Tear'. His records
were popular before the avuncular image he had developed by 1953

Ruby Murray (1955). A modest
girl whose every record was a hit

Domenico Modugno (1960). His 'Volare' was covered by many
other singers. It was the song, not the image, that did it

Slim Whitman (1955). An early photograph
taken after ' Rose Marie' had reached Number 1

Michael Holliday (1958). 'Story Of
My Life' was Number 1 for unassuming Mike

Peggy Lee (1961). Pictures of this jazz-based but inimitable
pop star were rare although her records were always hits

Joan Savage (1957). A queen of mime – she used her image to
promote other singers' records on a popular disc show of the day

Johnny Mathis (1959). An enduring record
maker, and he does it all with his voice alone

Helen Shapiro (1961). Not exactly without
an image, but her records were successful
before her first photographs were published

Bobby Darin (1960). He achieved a lot of sales before building
up his presentation. This was taken at the Palladium in London

The Everly Brothers (1960). Their blend of country and
rock brought massive record sales before they were ever seen

From Wax to Vinyl

During the fifties it was not uncommon to hear a presenter of gramophone records on radio – even on programmes as boringly intellectual and cultural as *Desert Island Discs* or *Down Your Way* – using the phrase, 'and this is their latest *waxing*'. Today the term is considered old-fashioned 'beat me daddy, eight to the bar' slang! Fashions change so fast in pop music that it is amazing to think that it has taken only 100 years since Bell introduced the first audible wax cylinder in 1886 for us to reach the world of micro-groove, stereo, video, laser, and soon holograph entertainment. People have preserved for posterity many sounds, albeit some discordant, by means of a variety of apparatus including wax, wire and tape, with records being pressed in a number of different materials.

Pop people have been involved in all these changes, but no period for them was as significant as the fifties, when record companies started to produce unprecedented numbers of single records in order to satisfy the public's new and increasing demand for novelty. The following pages show a few photographs, selected from many, of some of the survivors of pop who started making records in the years before the micro-groove – though not quite so far back as the days of wax – but whose sounds are still selling today. Included are some of the disc jockeys who helped them on the way – at least from shellac to vinyl.

Harry Belafonte (1958). The great calypso singer's
rendering of 'Boy Child' is an annual Christmas purchase

Anne Shelton (1957). This celebrated lady of pop
has had many chart successes during her long career

Tony Bennett (1956). An easy-going man who has been making hit records since 1952 and is a much sought-after cabaret star. This was taken behind the scenes at a London nightclub

Mario Lanza (1959). A rare working shot of a king among recording artistes. The usually eruptive singer posed quite readily for this, in a characteristic stance

Petula Clark (1956). Happy dressing-room picture at a first night

Tony Hancock (1954). His singing was not up to
standard, but his comedy programmes were something
else, and albums of them are still bought today.
He struck this pose just for the camera

Paul Anka (1957). A shot of the seventeen-year-old
snatched at the start of his first world tour

Dame Vera Lynn (1956). With her pearls and rose-trimmed
gown, Dame Vera was typical of the formal mid-fifties

Peter Sellers (1958). He always wanted to play the guitar

Spike Milligan (1957). A photograph taken in a room over
a greengrocer's shop at Shepherds Bush – the Goons'
first office, where they wrote their weekly radio scripts

Bing Crosby (1960). The hat, the coat over the music stand, the matchstick,
were all typical of Bing in the recording studio. This was shot in
Decca's Hampstead studios on a historic occasion when he recorded four songs

Judy Garland (1963). Although best known as a movie star, her
records featuring songs from various Hollywood musicals have
been selling since the thirties. This picture catches some
of the uncertainty and anguish that troubled the great star

All the DJs (1962). Photographed at a BBC Radio show called *Pop Inn*, this disc-dispensing line-up shows, left to right, Jack Jackson, Don Moss, Brian Mathew, Jimmy Young, Steve Race, Ken Sykora, David Gell, Sam Costa and Alan Dell

Jack Jackson (1960). A pioneer of pop record programmes, this ex-bandleader, together with his cat, began playing records on BBC Radio in about 1949 and later, in the fifties, took his zany television disc show into the ratings

Alan Freeman, Pete Murray and David Jacobs (1962).
Twisting at the Tin Pan Alley Ball

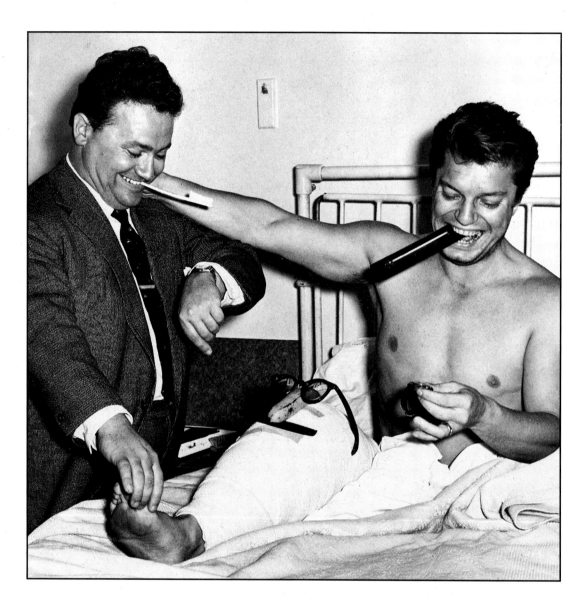

Harry Secombe (1957). Taking time off from the *Goon Show* to
visit Guy Mitchell who was in hospital. Mitchell had taken the old
show biz maxim seriously and broken his leg before going on stage

Shirley Bassey (1957). Making her television debut at the London Palladium

Sunday Night at the London Palladium

'If you've played the Palladium, you've arrived.' That is an old adage from the days of vaudeville, but it is still true today. There are some who say it is the most famous theatre in the world. Certainly, it is true to say that for every entertainer, musical or otherwise, it has always been considered the acme of achievement to tread the boards at the London Palladium.

Over the years countless shows have been presented at this celebrated venue, and many are the notables who have graced the number one dressing-room there, but no show was more popular or longer running than *Sunday Night at the London Palladium*. It was a live show screened by Associated Television featuring currently popular acts, and enabled several formerly obscure compères to rise to astral heights.

The main attraction of course was the Top of the Bill who was either the most popular television personality of the week, or whoever was Number 1 in the hit parade. Artistes of international repute were flown in weekly, happy in the knowledge that the exposure to some twenty million people could only increase their popularity. The show ran from 1955 to 1972.

Every Sunday evening for seven years I attended the dress rehearsal of *Sunday Night at the London Palladium* and have here reproduced some of the many celebrities that I photographed there.

Bruce Forsyth and Sammy Davies Jnr (1961). Demonstrating
their vocal and pedantic abilities for the camera during rehearsal

David Whitfield (1956). Onstage
with the Palladium Tiller Girls.
His 'Cara Mia', made with
Mantovani and his Orchestra, went gold

Winifred Atwell (1957). Seen here with the old
upright piano that she played on all her hit records

Nat King Cole (1960). Topping the bill on one of many occasions

Stanley Holloway (1960). He is
still popular with record buyers
everywhere for his many
albums of songs and monologues

Jo Stafford (1957). Formerly a
singer with Tommy Dorsey's band.
By 1955 she had sold more than
twenty-five million singles

Kay Starr (1960). 'Rock and Roll
Waltz' was the unlikely title
of her most successful single,
an international Number 1 in 1956

Howard Keel (1958). Despite his
success in Hollywood musicals, he
was never very animated at the
microphone; the voice was sufficient

Eartha Kitt (1957). Her wavering vocal sound and sultry
style put her in the Top Twenty and also top of the bill

Jane Russell (1959). She had recording contracts with
Decca and MGM for several years and sang in some of
her movies, but she never topped the Hit Parade

The characteristic revolving stage finale of
Sunday Night at the London Palladium, taken in 1960

Eve Boswell and Paul Robeson (1962).
'Evergreen Eve', an international cabaret
star who can sing and record in fourteen
different languages, photographed
with the fabled baritone in the star
dressing-room of the London Palladium
when they appeared on the same bill

Rosemary Clooney (1961).
She had many Number 1
hits but her main interests
were her children and
her husband Jose Ferrer

Judy Garland (1963). 'Worried in the wings, but stupendous onstage' was my impression of this eternally famous singer on an unforgettable *Sunday Night*

The Platters (1960). The lead tenor voice of Tony Williams
is a well remembered feature of such hits as 'The Great
Pretender' and 'Only You'. His fellow Platters are, from the
left, Herbert Reed, David Lynch, Zola Taylor and Paul Robi

Pat Boone (1962). A very co-operative 'all-American boy' who appeared
several times at the London Palladium, with a string of hits to sing

Jane Morgan (1959). On a
full stage set to present
the current Number 1
song – 'The Day
The Rains Came'

Breakthrough

'The Corporation would never agree to it – not a whole programme devoted to that sort of music. It's degenerate and could lead young people into trouble.' This typical quote from a BBC executive in the year 1956 referred to a new and exciting style of pop music which was currently sweeping America but which in Britain was regarded with contempt by record producers, disc jockeys and musicians alike. Based on the original rhythm and blues expressions of musicians from the southern states of America and introduced, visually as well as audibly, to the rest of the world by Elvis Presley, the style was really launched commercially by Bill Haley. The new 'rough edge' music and its idols offered something which was exclusive to teenagers. They guarded it jealously and called it rock 'n' roll.

Reluctantly but inevitably British radio and television had to acknowledge the demand by young people for some musical outlet of their own, and so began the gradual capitulation resulting in BBC TV's *6.5 Special*. A sort of forerunner of *Top of the Pops*, it started in 1957 and at least gave budding young guitar strummers and singers a chance to be seen by the adolescents who were buying their records. There was still a lot of restraint about the show, however, and also confusion, with skiffle music dominating the fearsome rock 'n' roll trend.

The last hurdle was overcome in the following year, when ABC Television transmitted its controversial *Oh Boy!* show, directed by the now legendary Jack Good. The series was watched with relief by the younger generation as the pillars of establishment collapsed in an eruption of driving new music and defiant posturing, some of which I captured in the following photographs.

Cliff Richard (1957). My first portrait of this incomparable pop star

Ray Ellington and
Marion Ryan (1957).
A shot taken at one of
BBC Radio's concerts at
the Albert Hall – complete
with script in hand!

BBC Television's new programme *6.5 Special* (1957)

Don Lang (1957). He was featured weekly on
6.5 Special with his Frantic Five

Lonnie Donegan (1957). Vocalist,
instrumentalist and entertainer – once voted
one of Britain's 'Top Ten Best-Dressed Men'

6.5 Special (1958). The Mudlarks perform
for a slightly self-conscious audience

Jim Dale (1957). He made his debut on *6.5 Special*
where he had a weekly spot. Broadway is his scene today

Laurie London (1958). Another singer from *6.5 Special*.
This fourteen-year-old sold a million

Oh Boy! (1958). This panoramic shot shows clockwise from left: the Cutters, the Vernons Girls, the Dallas Boys, Lord Rockingham's Eleven, with Benny Green behind dark glasses and Bill Forbes on the front mike

Left: Duane Eddy and Bert Weedon (1960). Two top guitar exponents meet in London

Right: Conway Twitty (1958). Guesting on *Oh Boy!*

Left: The last *Oh Boy!* show (1959). A group shot taken quickly, off-stage, when producer Jack Good gave everyone a three-minute break. Left to right, back row: two Dallas Boys, Bill Forbes, Peter Elliot, Marty Wilde, Don Storer, Cliff Richard, Mike Preston, Billy Fury, Cuddly Dudley and Red Price. Front row: three Dallas Boys, Cherry Wainer, Lorie Mann, Dickie Pride, Don Lang, Neville Taylor and one of the Cutters

Wee Willie Harris (1958). An important milestoner in the
history of pop people: with his pink hair and exaggerated gear,
he was the first to exploit the visual image to the full

Cliff Richard (1958).
Above: A photograph taken
to mark the occasion of
Cliff and the Shadows'
first record for EMI.
Left to right: A & R man
Norrie Paramor, Cliff
Richard, Jet Harris,
Tony Meehan, Hank
Marvin and Bruce Welch

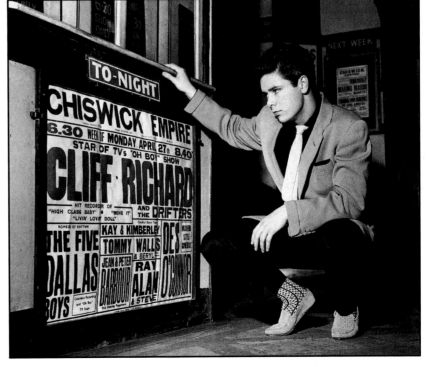

Right: In 1958 Cliff
also got top billing
for the first time

Rock Arrival

Today it is fashionable to refer to everyone and everything connected with popular music as 'rock'. This unseemly word is used almost worshipfully when discussing any music which is beyond the periphery of the London Symphony Orchestra. Every singer is a 'rock singer', every musician is a 'rock musician'; there are rock concerts, rock DJs, rock programmes on radio and television, rock managers and agents, rock columns in newspapers and magazines, and A to Zs of Rock. But little remains today of the original rock 'n' roll music that was born in the fifties. Thought to be exciting then, perhaps it would not now be violent enough to go with today's way of life.

From 1958 for about five years rock 'n' roll was the top attraction in Britain for record-buyers and live show followers – but it was not to last. By the end of the fifties Elvis Presley had long since given up making rock 'n' roll records and was singing ballads and acting in movies. Many other American exponents were either lost, had changed their style or turned to religion. Established singers were not sure how to cut their next record. This confusion didn't last long. New leaders soon emerged, beginning with the Beatles.

Marty Wilde (1957). Caught in the spotlight which
is still with him, but which is now shared with his daughter

Suzi Miller (1957). First British girl singer to record in
the rock 'n' roll style. She was little known in the
fifties but with the reissue of her records is recognized now

Bill Haley (1957). The real pioneer of rock 'n' roll who
shook the pop world with his first record. Photographed
backstage at the Dominion Theatre, Tottenham Court Road, London

Tommy Steele (1958).
Seen here with the Dallas
Boys. The slightly bent
knees, the clicking fingers,
collars, ties, and wide
trousers sum up the
style of this period

Jess Conrad (1959). One of
the few good actors to emerge
from pop stars of this period

Charlie Gracie (1959).
'Butterfly' was a Number 1
for this American artiste,
but he ended his career in
rock suddenly and voluntarily

Jet Harris (1961). Irrational
star of the bass guitar who
never came to terms with success

Buddy Holly (1958). A photograph taken during his brief tour of England in 1958

Eden Kane (1961). Kane figured high in the
scream ratings this year with 'Well I Ask You'

Adam Faith (1960). Pop star, writer, actor, agent
and manager, seen here in action in his early days

John Leyton (1960). His rock career
was a stepping stone to success in films

Shane Fenton (1961). He found fame
in the seventies as Alvin Stardust

Eddie Cochran (1960). Remembered by rock fans
throughout the world for catching the mood of an unsettled
teenage generation at the end of the fifties. Here
he is onstage at the annual *NME* Poll Winners' Concert

Jerry Lee Lewis (1959). Admirable keyboard-pounding
rocker whose concerts and shows have continued
unabated to the present day. A rock conservationist

Gene Vincent (1960). Another classic
American artiste, who is still revered
as one of the top exponents of rock

Billy Fury (1962).
One of the vanguard of
'rebel' idols of the early
sixties. Many still pay
homage to the late singer,
maintaining his cult
image as Britain's
king of pop 'n' rock

The Everly Brothers (1961).
Onstage with the Crickets
(from left, Joe Mauldin,
Jerry Allison, Sonny
Curtis), who backed them
for their UK tour

The Beatles (1963). Happy days in the dressing-room
with Roy Orbison and Gerry and the Pacemakers
Right: Slightly self-conscious in their new suits

Index of Artistes